Explore the Universe
STARS— BIRTH AND DEATH

WORLD BOOK

a Scott Fetzer company
Chicago
www.worldbookonline.com

World Book, Inc.
233 N. Michigan Avenue
Chicago, IL 60601
U.S.A.

For information about other World Book publications, visit our
Web site at **http://www.worldbookonline.com** or call
1-800-WORLDBK (967-5325).

For information about sales to schools and
libraries, call **1-800-975-3250 (United States),**
or **1-800-837-5365 (Canada).**

Library of Congress Cataloging-in-Publication data
Stars-- birth and death.
    p. cm. -- (Explore the universe)
    Includes index.
    Summary: "An introduction to stars with information about
their formation and life cycle. Includes diagrams, fun facts,
glossary, resource list, and index"--Provided by publisher.
    ISBN: 978-0-7166-9548-6
    1. Stars--Juvenile literature. 2. Stars--Evolution--Juvenile
literature. I. World Book, Inc. I. Series.
    QB801.7.S725 2010
    523.8--dc22
                            2009042581

ISBN: 978-0-7166-9544-8 (set)
Printed in China by Leo Paper Products, LTD.,
  Heshan, Guangdong
1st printing February 2010

STAFF
Executive Committee:
President: Paul A. Gazzolo
Vice President and Chief Marketing Officer:
  Patricia Ginnis
Vice President and Chief Financial Officer:
  Donald D. Keller
Vice President and Editor in Chief: Paul A. Kobasa
Vice President, Licensing & Business Development:
  Richard Flower
Managing Director, International: Benjamin Hinton
Director, Human Resources: Bev Ecker
Chief Technology Officer: Tim Hardy

Editorial:
Associate Director, Supplementary Publications:
  Scott Thomas
Managing Editor, Supplementary Publications:
  Barbara A. Mayes
Senior Editor, Supplementary Publications:
  Kristina A. Vaicikonis
Manager, Research, Supplementary Publications:
  Cheryl Graham
Manager, Contracts & Compliance
  (Rights & Permissions): Loranne K. Shields
Editors: Michael DuRoss, Brian Johnson
Writer: Robert N. Knight
Indexer: David Pofelski

Graphics and Design:
Manager: Tom Evans
Coordinator, Design Development
  and Production: Brenda B. Tropinski
Associate Designer: Matt Carrington
Contributing Photographs Editor: Carol Parden

Pre-Press and Manufacturing:
Director: Carma Fazio
Manufacturing Manager: Steven K. Hueppchen
Production/Technology Manager: Anne Fritzinger
Proofreader: Emilie Schrage

Cover image:
The glowing core of a star that exploded
about 10,000 years ago appears to ride
above a cloud of dust and gas known as
the Witch's Broom Nebula. Surrounding
gas molecules excited by the rapidly
expanding cloud give the nebula its
brilliant colors.

NASA/T. A. Rector (U. Alaska),
NOAO, AURA, NSF

CONTENTS

If a word is printed in **bold letters that look like this,** that word's meaning is given in the glossary on pages 60-61.

INTRODUCTION

On any clear night, people can look up at a sky filled with thousands of twinkling stars. These stars seem eternal and unchanging. But if we could peer a billion years into the future, some stars would no longer shine, while we might notice new stars shining where once there was only darkness.

In truth, each star has a life span. A star is born, it matures, and then it dies. The manner of a star's life and death depends on how much fuel is available to keep the star shining. Smaller stars burn out and drift through the heavens as dark remains. The largest stars explode with tremendous violence. Their remains seed the cosmos with heavy elements, including those needed by living things. The shock waves they generate in death cause the birth of new stars, starting another cycle of birth and death among the stars.

Hundreds of newborn stars surround a group of four massive stars (center), each more than 100,000 times as bright as the sun, in the Orion Nebula. This false-color image was made using infrared, ultraviolet, and visible-light data from the Hubble and Spitzer space telescopes.

The sun is a **star.** It provides light and heat to the planets in the **solar system.** Life on Earth could not survive without the sun.

Stars vary in size, color, and brightness. Some are thousands of times brighter than the sun, shining brilliant blue. Others give off only a fraction of the sun's light, gleaming dark red.

INSIDE A GIANT

Through most of their lives, stars are made of an extremely hot, gas-like substance called **plasma.** There is nothing solid inside most stars. Rather, stars churn with mighty currents of plasma. Deep inside the star, a central region called the **core** is crushed by the immense weight of all the plasma above. The core's temperature is so high that it could instantly melt any material.

ATOMIC SUNLIGHT

The intense conditions inside the star's core smash together atoms, the tiny particles that make up ordinary matter. Their *nuclei* (cores) *fuse* (join) to form new, larger nuclei in a process called **nuclear fusion.** Nuclear fusion provides the tremendous energy given off by stars. The sunlight that warms your shoulders on a summer day is the product of nuclear fusion deep inside the sun.

A star is a huge, shining ball in space that gives off tremendous amounts of visible light and other forms of energy.

Stars are born in great clouds of dust and gas, such as this nebula near the star Antares.

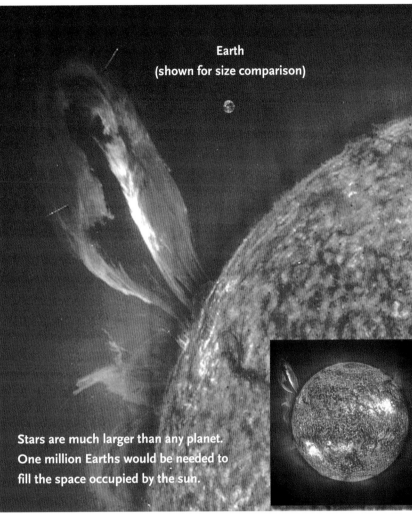

Earth
(shown for size comparison)

Stars are much larger than any planet. One million Earths would be needed to fill the space occupied by the sun.

DID YOU KNOW?

There are fewer grains of sand on all of Earth's beaches than there are stars in the universe. Our galaxy contains hundreds of billions of stars, and the universe contains billions or even trillions of galaxies like ours.

DO STARS LAST FOREVER?

THE FUSION ENGINE

The **stars** seem unchanging to us because most people live for less than 100 years, while most stars live for billions of years. As long as a star contains enough fuel to continue **nuclear fusion,** it remains stable. Younger stars are made mostly of **hydrogen,** the lightest **chemical element.** This hydrogen serves as fuel. Stars produce energy by *fusing* (combining) hydrogen into **helium,** a slightly heavier chemical element. As a star runs out of hydrogen, it must begin to fuse helium into even heavier elements, such as carbon and oxygen.

STELLAR OLD AGE

Stars go through tremendous changes as they near the end of their lives. As nuclear fusion in a star shifts to heavier elements, the star becomes unstable. Eventually, the star becomes a **red giant** or **red supergiant,** swelling up like a red balloon. Smaller stars slowly shed their

DID YOU KNOW?

Scientists believe that a star called HE0107-5240 is among the oldest stars in the Milky Way. They estimate it is more than 13 billion years old—nearly as old as the universe itself.

As a star enters the last stages of its life, it may throw off its outer atmosphere, creating colorful streams of gas, such as these from the Butterfly Nebula.

Stars do not last forever. But most stars live for billions of years.

outer layers, leaving a small, hot core called a **white dwarf.** Larger stars may die with tremendous violence, exploding in a **supernova.**

THE SUN'S MIDDLE AGE

Scientists believe that the sun was born about 4.6 billion years ago and will live for at least another 5 billion years. Thus, the sun is in the middle of its life. Eventually, the sun will expand into a giant red ball and burn up the inner planets, possibly including Earth. In the end, nothing will remain of the sun but a white dwarf. Over billions of years, the white dwarf will cool to a **black dwarf,** the dark remnant of a once mighty star.

Near the end of their lives, stars brighten and become redder in color.

WHERE DID THE FIRST STARS COME FROM?

According to the **big bang** theory, about 13.7 billion years ago, the entire universe occupied only a single point. That point exploded, starting the expansion of the universe. In fact, the universe is still expanding today.

THE BIRTH OF STARS

In the beginning, the universe was filled with energy. As the universe expanded, the first **chemical elements** began to form. Most of this matter was **hydrogen,** spread thinly throughout the universe. However, there were clumps in this early matter, where the hydrogen was concentrated. These clumps of hydrogen developed into the first **stars.**

STAR STUFF

Through **nuclear fusion,** the first stars produced the heavier elements, including carbon and oxygen. At the end of their lives, the largest of these stars exploded, flinging the elements essential to life out into space. These

Galaxies in shapes and colors both familiar and new to astronomers appear in an image of the oldest—and farthest—galaxies ever seen in visible light, taken by the Hubble Space Telescope. Some of the galaxies formed in the first billion years after the big bang.

Scientists believe that the universe began in a cosmic event called the big bang. About 200 million years later, the first stars formed from the hot gas produced by this event.

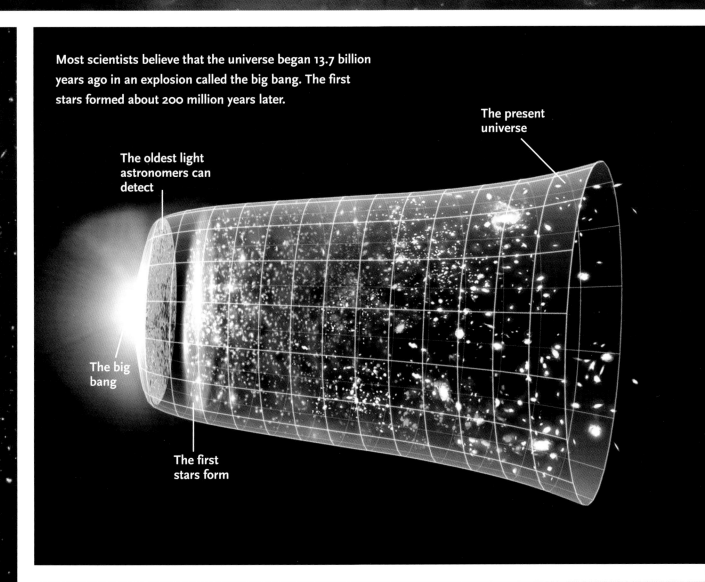

Most scientists believe that the universe began 13.7 billion years ago in an explosion called the big bang. The first stars formed about 200 million years later.

The present universe

The oldest light astronomers can detect

The big bang

The first stars form

elements joined the dust and gas that became new stars, including the sun.

On Earth, there is little hydrogen compared with other chemical elements, and that is a good thing. Life could not exist without such elements as carbon and oxygen.

We can thank the first stars for providing these heavier elements. Many of the elements that form our bodies were born inside stars. As the American astronomer Carl Sagan said, "We are all star stuff."

THE LONG LIVES OF STARS

Different stages of a star's life appear in an image of the nebula NGC 3603 taken by the Hubble Space Telescope. Clouds of gas (right) are collapsing to form new stars. Bright, hot blue stars (center) have blasted away nearby material, ending star formation in the immediate area. The blue supergiant Sher 25 (upper left) is throwing off great blobs of gas. Scientists believe that Sher 25, which has 60 times the mass of the sun, may explode in a supernova within a few thousand years. The gas thrown off by Sher 25 may one day become part of new stars.

Sher 25

Blobs of gas thrown off by Sher 25

Massive, short-lived blue stars

A star is born in a clump of dust and gas within a nebula. Over time, the gravitational pull of this clump attracts more matter until a glowing, hot body called a protostar forms. When nuclear fusion begins in the core of the protostar, it becomes a T-Tauri star. The newborn star throws off much of its surrounding material. Some of the material may collect in chunks called planetesimals. As the star becomes mature, planetesimals may combine to form planets.

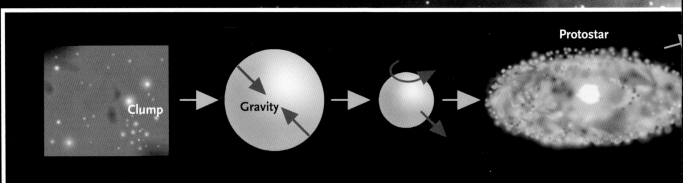

Clump

Gravity

Protostar

Massive newborn stars in the Large
Magellanic Cloud (above) turn the
surrounding gas blue with their powerful
radiation. The gas was once part of a
large cloud that collapsed to form the
stars. These stars are now pushing away
the gas, ending a period of star birth.

T-Tauri star

Planetesimal

Gas
jets

Young star
with planets

If you look up at the night sky, you will see only the tiny pinpoints of light that are **stars** and **planets.** However, if we look with a telescope, we can also make out hazy blobs that resemble clouds. These clouds are enormous bodies of dust and gas. Such a cloud is called a **nebula;** two or more clouds are called nebulae.

STELLAR NURSERIES

Most stars are born inside nebulae. Star formation begins when a shock wave from a stellar explosion or other disturbance passes through the nebula. The disturbance causes dust and gas to clump together. After millions of years, the dust and gas may collapse into a ball and form a brightly shining star. Some nebulae contain enough dust and gas to give birth to 100,000 stars like the sun. In stellar nurseries such as the Great Nebula in Orion, we can observe thousands of newborn stars.

BORN IN THE MILKY WAY

In 2006, scientists used a space observatory to study sections of our **galaxy** with high levels of a certain form of aluminum. This form of aluminum is produced in massive star explosions called **supernovae.** The scientists estimated from their observations that about seven new stars are born in the Milky Way Galaxy each year.

Glowing balls of gaseous iron, called the Orion bullets, trailed by streamers of hydrogen gas, explode from the Orion Nebula at speeds of more than 250 miles (400 kilometers) per second. Astronomers have linked the ejection of the bullets to an unknown event that led to the formation of a group of massive stars.

Stars are born in clouds of dust
and gas called nebulae.

In the 1700's, the French astronomer
Charles Messier created one of the
first catalogs of nebulae.

Newborn stars are surrounded by
disks of dust and gas in an image
of the Orion Nebula taken by the
Hubble Space Telescope.

ARE THERE DIFFERENT KINDS OF NEBULAE?

A **nebula** is a huge cloud of dust and gas. However, not all nebulae are alike.

TRUE NEBULAE

There are three kinds of true nebulae, including **emission nebulae, reflection nebulae,** and **dark nebulae.**

An emission nebula glows in a way that resembles a fluorescent lamp. This type of nebula glows because it is near an extremely hot, bright **star.** The **electromagnetic radiation** given off by this star causes gas in the nebula to glow. Electromagnetic radiation includes the entire range of light, both visible and invisible. We can see **visible light,** though such forms of light as **infrared rays, ultraviolet rays,** and **X rays** are invisible to us.

A reflection nebula glows more faintly than an emission nebula. A reflection nebula is typically found near a smaller, cooler star. The star's electromagnetic radiation is not strong enough to cause the nebula's gas to glow. However, the nebula's dust particles reflect the star's light, causing a weaker glow.

In a dark nebula, no stars are close enough to cause the nebula to glow. A dark nebula may even block light from stars behind it, creating a black patch in space.

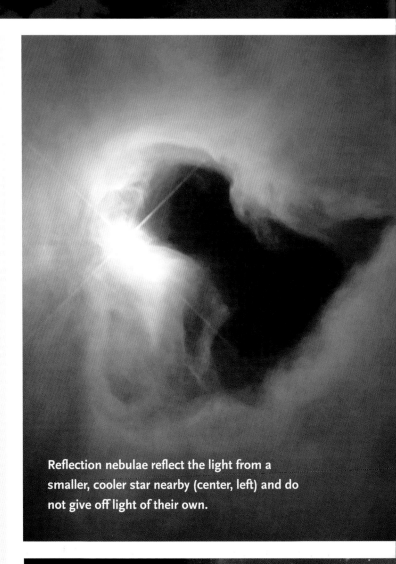

Reflection nebulae reflect the light from a smaller, cooler star nearby (center, left) and do not give off light of their own.

DID YOU KNOW?

The Orion Nebula, located on the sword of the constellation Orion, is the brightest nebula in Earth's night sky.

STELLAR REMAINS

Planetary nebulae are unlike true nebulae. They are typically smaller, with a round shape. A planetary nebula forms when an aging star begins to collapse and throw off the outer layers of its atmosphere. These layers of atmosphere spread out over time, forming the nebula. The hot core of the dying star causes the nebula to glow.

Early astronomers thought these nebulae looked like planets, inspiring the name. Although these nebulae have nothing to do with planets, astronomers still use the traditional name.

Dark nebulae absorb light, creating dark blots in space.

Emission nebulae glow much like a fluorescent lamp, as radiation from a bright star excites the nebula's gas.

Stars—Birth and Death 17

NEBULAE— CLOUDS OF THE COSMOS

The Boomerang Nebula (background image) is in the constellation Centaurus, about 5,000 light-years from Earth. The nebula was formed over the last 1,500 years as the star at its center threw off vast quantities of gas, equal to about 1.5 times the mass of the sun. A star may throw off the outer layers of its atmosphere as it nears the end of life.

The Witch Head Nebula, known formally as IC 2118, is found in the constellation Orion (the Hunter). Tiny grains of dust in the nebula reflect blue light from the bright star Rigel (above, center). Rigel forms one of the "feet" of Orion, shining 40,000 times as brightly as the sun. At the end of its life, Rigel will likely explode. The shock wave that follows will cause dust and gas in the Witch Head Nebula to collapse, forming new stars.

Massive columns of dust and gas light-years long project from the Eagle Nebula. The columns are called "the pillars of creation" because they are filled with newborn stars.

A closer image of a column in the Eagle Nebula shows how bright stars cause gas in the nebula to glow.

Most **stars** develop from matter inside **nebulae.** The dust and gas in a nebula are usually thinly spread and extremely cold. A nebula may remain cold and dark for millions or even billions of years.

STELLAR DEATH, STELLAR BIRTH

When massive stars die, they explode in a **supernova** that sends a shock wave through space. If this shock wave or some other disturbance passes through a nebula, the long process of stellar birth may begin. As the shock wave passes through the dust and gas, it pushes these materials together into dense pockets. The pull of **gravity** soon draws matter in these pockets even closer together. Soon, all the dust and gas in the area is falling in on one central region, where a new star will be born.

A SPINNING, GLOWING BALL

As material falls in on the central region, the dust and gas begin to rotate. This rotation

Radiation from bright stars can push dust and gas together, forming clumps that may become new stars.

The dying red giant star Mira (far right) speeds through the Milky Way, trailing a comet-like tail of ejected gas and dust 13 light-years long. Dense "lumps" in the tail may one day develop into new stars.

causes the growing ball at the center to rotate as well. As the central region pulls material in tighter, it spins more rapidly, in the same way that a spinning skater rotates faster if she pulls in her arms.

The gravitational pull of the central body becomes stronger as its **mass** grows. Mass is the amount of matter in an object. The increasing gravity compresses material in the ball, increasing its density. The pressure and temperature in the ball grow as well. The thick clouds of surrounding dust and gas hold in heat rather than allowing the heat to radiate into space. This helps the temperature to increase further. Eventually, the ball can shrink no further and begins to glow with heat. Where once there was a thin cloud of dust and gas, there is now a glowing, rotating ball. The ball has become a **protostar.**

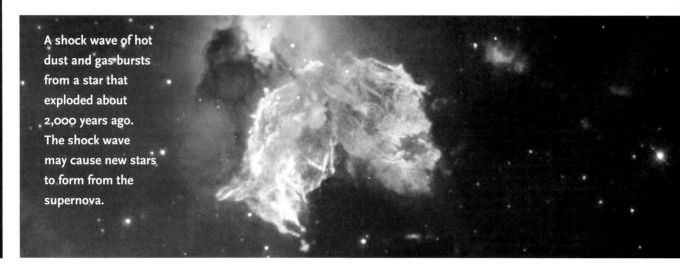

A shock wave of hot dust and gas bursts from a star that exploded about 2,000 years ago. The shock wave may cause new stars to form from the supernova.

Dust and gas continue to fall into the ball of material forming in the **nebula.** When the ball's growing heat exerts enough pressure to prevent further collapse, it has become a **protostar.**

THE INWARD SPIRAL

It typically takes about 100,000 years from the time that the clump of dust and gas inside the nebula began spinning and contracting to the point at which it has become a protostar. The protostar is now very hot, with a surface temperature of perhaps 4,000 Kelvin (K) (6,700 °F).

By comparison, the dust and gas from which the protostar formed may have been only 10 K (440 °F).

Although the protostar has become a stable body, it continues to contract as it adds **mass** (amount of matter). The surrounding dust and gas form a disk called an **accretion disk,** which continues to spiral inward, feeding the growing protostar. The protostar typically doubles in mass and then doubles again. Some material in the accretion disk may eventually become planets, comets, and asteroids surrounding the newborn star.

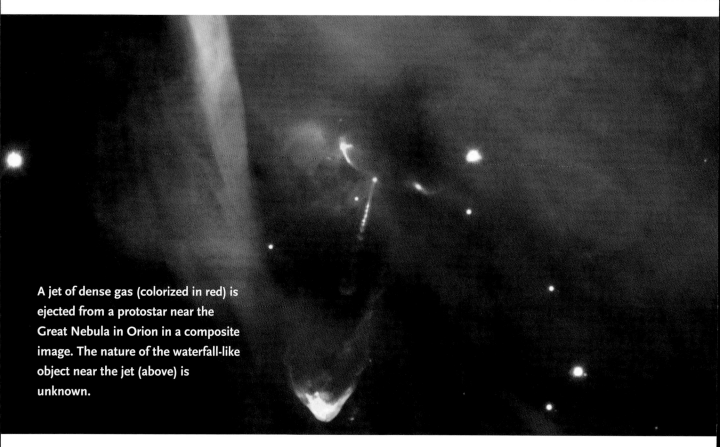

A jet of dense gas (colorized in red) is ejected from a protostar near the Great Nebula in Orion in a composite image. The nature of the waterfall-like object near the jet (above) is unknown.

A protostar is a hot, glowing ball of gas. It is the final stage before the birth of a star.

Jet

Protostar

Protoplanetary disk

Jet

Hot, narrow jets of electrically charged particles from a protostar's dusty cocoon stream from the protostar's poles (above) in an artist's illustration. Moving at speeds of thousands of miles per hour, these jets may extend for trillions of miles into space. They form as the inner parts of a planetary disk rub against the magnetic field of a protostar.

A protostar, planetary disk, and trademark jets (above) emerge from a cocoon of dust and gas in the Orion Nebula. By this stage, much of the original material in the disk as well as in the protostar's dusty cocoon has been added to the star or blown away by the jets.

HOW DOES A PROTOSTAR BECOME A TRUE STAR?

What happens next to a **protostar** depends upon its **mass** (amount of matter). A small protostar may fall short of becoming a true star and end up as a **brown dwarf.** A brown dwarf is basically an intermediate step between large planets and small stars.

THE BIRTH OF A STAR

Protostars with enough mass go on to become true stars. When the temperature inside the **core** reaches 10 million Kelvin (1.8 million °F), **nuclear fusion** of **hydrogen** begins. This moment marks the true birth of the star. Nuclear fusion releases tremendous amounts of energy. The star shines brightly, producing visible and invisible **electromagnetic radiation.** Between the formation of the protostar and the birth of the true star, millions of years have passed.

A newborn *binary* (two-star) system near the constellation Taurus (the Bull), known as T-Tauri, has given its name to all similar young star systems. The central regions of the stars are expected to become hot enough to trigger nuclear fusion within a few million years.

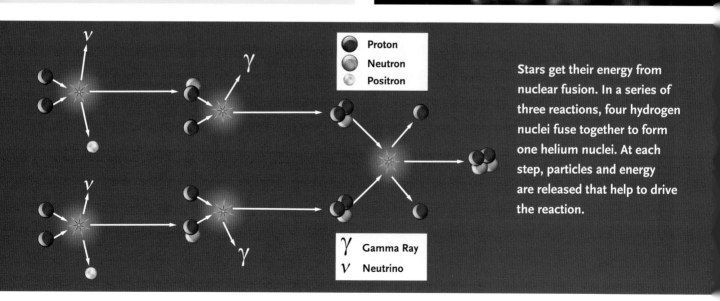

●	Proton
◐	Neutron
○	Positron

γ	Gamma Ray
ν	Neutrino

Stars get their energy from nuclear fusion. In a series of three reactions, four hydrogen nuclei fuse together to form one helium nuclei. At each step, particles and energy are released that help to drive the reaction.

A protostar becomes a true star when its core becomes hot enough to support nuclear fusion.

A newborn star is called a **T-Tauri star.** The star begins to produce a **stellar wind.** The stellar wind is made up of energetic particles blasted away from the star's atmosphere. The stellar wind and the star's radiation begin to push away the remaining dust and gas in the surrounding **accretion disk.** In many cases, the disk channels the stellar wind into two jets, each at a right angle to the disk.

The T-Tauri star continues to contract for another 10 million years. It stops contracting when the energy produced by fusion in its core balances the force of gravity pushing it to contract. By this time, hydrogen fusion in the core is supplying all the star's energy. It has now reached a stage called the **main sequence.**

The stellar wind of newborn star LL Ori creates a *bow shock* (type of shock wave) in the gas of the Great Nebula in Orion. The stellar wind drives away gas, preventing further growth of the star.

Stars vary widely in surface temperature, brightness, color, size, and other factors. However, for all their differences, most stars are on the **main sequence.** A main-sequence star produces its energy from **nuclear fusion** of **hydrogen** in its **core.** Stars spend the middle part of their lives on the main sequence.

THE H-R DIAGRAM

Astronomers have created a graph that helps us visualize the main sequence. It is called the **Hertzsprung-Russell (H-R) diagram.** The H-R diagram helps us to understand how astronomers classify stars. **Luminosity,** or brightness, is marked on the *vertical* (left) scale. Surface temperature is marked on the *horizontal* (bottom) scale.

For stars fusing hydrogen in their core, surface temperature and luminosity are closely matched—the higher the temperature, the higher the luminosity. Main-sequence stars, near the upper left in the diagram, are the hottest and brightest stars. Stars near the bottom right are the coolest and darkest.

The sun is on the main sequence. When the sun runs out of hydrogen in its core, it will leave the main sequence.

OFF THE MAIN SEQUENCE

Stars at the beginning or the end of their lives do not produce their energy from fusing hydrogen in the core. Such stars are not on the main sequence. **White dwarfs** are in the lower left corner of the H-R diagram. Although their temperature remains high, their luminosity is much lower. **Red giants** and **red supergiants** are in the upper right corner of the H-R diagram. Although their luminosity remains high, their surface temperature has fallen.

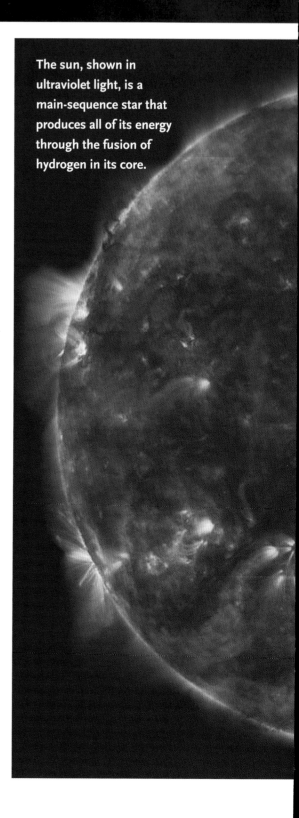

The sun, shown in ultraviolet light, is a main-sequence star that produces all of its energy through the fusion of hydrogen in its core.

A main-sequence star produces all its energy from hydrogen fusion in the core. A main-sequence star is in the middle part of its life.

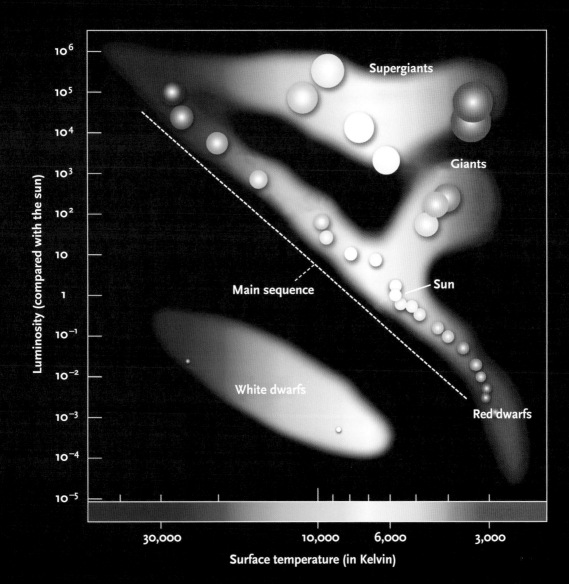

A graph known as the Hertzsprung-Russell diagram charts stars according to their *luminosity* (rate of energy output) and surface temperature. About 90 percent of the stars we can see fall in a roughly diagonal band on the diagram that stretches from low luminosity and temperature to high luminosity and temperature. Astronomers call this band the main sequence. Throughout the main sequence, luminosity and *mass* (amount of matter) generally increase with surface temperature; that is, more massive main-sequence stars tend to have hotter surfaces and give off more energy than less massive ones.

Disks of gas and dust that may one day develop into planets surround four young stars in the Orion Nebula, in an image taken by the Hubble Space Telescope.

Not all stars have planets, but astronomers believe that many, if not most, stars do. Astronomers have only begun finding planets around distant stars.

Astronomers have discovered hundreds of *exoplanets* (planets orbiting stars other than the sun). Among them is a large planet circling the red dwarf star VB 10, about 20 light-years away from Earth, shown in an artist's illustration. The planet is likely similar in size to Jupiter but orbits much closer to its star.

We are familiar with the sun and the **solar system.** Eight **planets** orbit around the sun, along with millions of other smaller objects, such as dwarf planets, asteroids, and comets. Earth is the planet we know best.

People have long asked whether other **stars** may have their own **planetary systems.** They have long wondered whether life might exist on distant worlds.

Finding planets around distant stars is a difficult task. A planet is small compared with a star, and it reflects only a tiny fraction of the star's light. Until recently, astronomers had no proof of the existence of **exoplanets,** or planets beyond the solar system.

THE SEARCH FOR EXOPLANETS

By the 1990's, astronomers had more-sensitive telescopes, as well as bigger and faster computers. With the aid of these tools, scientists began to detect planets around distant stars.

By the end of 2009, astronomers had discovered more than 400 exoplanets. Most of the exoplanets discovered so far are large gaseous planets that resemble Jupiter. However, most of these planets orbit much closer to their star than Jupiter does. Such planets are unlikely to harbor life as we know it. However, there is no reason to think most exoplanets are large, hot planets of this kind. Scientists have found such exoplanets simply because large planets orbiting near to their central star are the easiest to detect. In time, scientists expect to find many rocky planets that resemble Earth.

WHAT IS A BROWN DWARF?

A **star** on the **main sequence** shines because of the **nuclear fusion** in its **core.** A star can only support fusion at incredibly high temperatures, which can only be achieved if the star reaches a sufficient **mass** (amount of matter). A **brown dwarf** does not have sufficient mass to sustain nuclear fusion.

STARS THAT FIZZLE

Some **protostars** are never able to gather enough mass to become true stars. Such protostars reach high temperatures and even glow as they collect gas and dust. But they do not have enough mass to sustain nuclear fusion. The protostar eventually becomes cool and dark. Scientists call such a failed star a brown dwarf.

BETWEEN PLANETS AND STARS

Scientists believe that most brown dwarfs are about the same size as the solar system's largest planet, Jupiter. Jupiter is more than 11 times as wide as Earth. However, brown dwarfs have from 13 to 75 times the mass of Jupiter. This means that brown dwarfs are much denser than planets.

Brown dwarfs are extremely difficult to detect because they are so dim. As with planets, their faint, reflected light is usually blotted out by the light of nearby stars. In fact, it was not until 1995 that astronomers were sure they had found one. Nevertheless, scientists believe that the number of brown dwarfs in the universe is similar to the number of stars. If so, there are trillions.

Two brown dwarfs in a binary star system (green dots in upper left of image) orbit a sun-like star. Together, the brown dwarfs have only 11 percent the mass of the sun.

A brown dwarf is an intermediate step between a planet and a star. It is a protostar that has too little mass to become a true star.

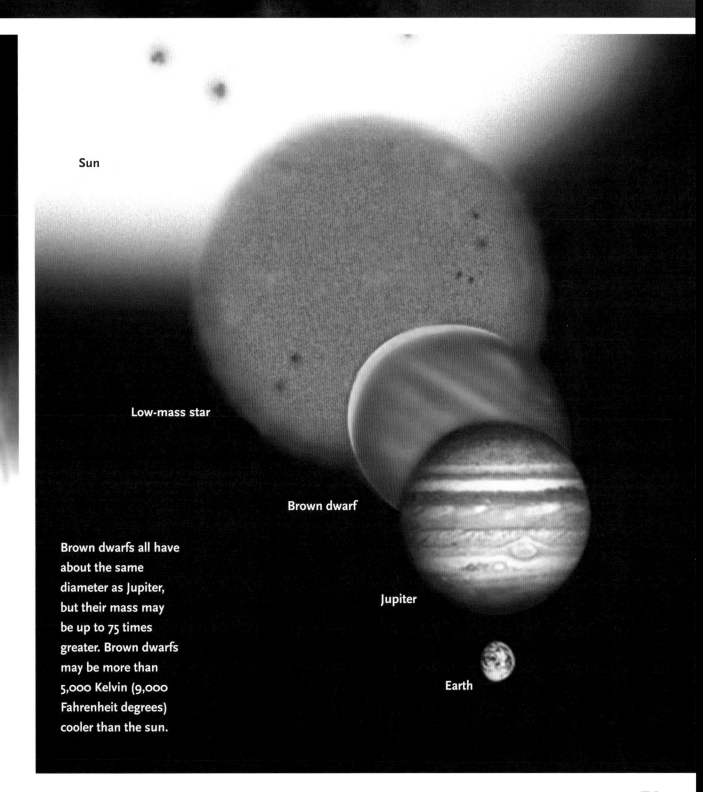

Sun

Low-mass star

Brown dwarf

Brown dwarfs all have about the same diameter as Jupiter, but their mass may be up to 75 times greater. Brown dwarfs may be more than 5,000 Kelvin (9,000 Fahrenheit degrees) cooler than the sun.

Jupiter

Earth

BECOMING A GIANT

When a **star** has converted all the **hydrogen** in its **core** into **helium,** violent changes take place. Much higher temperatures are required for **nuclear fusion** to convert helium into heavier **chemical elements.** As the fusion of hydrogen in the core fails, the entire star begins to contract. This contraction causes the temperature of the star's interior to increase rapidly.

The temperature becomes so high that hydrogen fusion begins in a thin shell surrounding the core. This fusion produces even more energy than was produced by hydrogen fusion in the core. The additional energy pushes against the star's outer layers, so the star expands enormously. As the star expands, its outermost layers cool considerably, giving the star a red appearance. The star has now left the **main sequence** and become a **red giant.** A star with a great **mass** (amount of matter) will become a **red supergiant.**

DEATH THROES

The star now uses up its remaining fuel at a relatively rapid rate. Low-mass stars like the sun gradually blast away their outer layers. In time, nothing but the hot core remains. Without fuel, fusion in the core ends, leaving behind a **white dwarf.** The white dwarf slowly cools to become a **black dwarf.**

Stars with high mass do not die quietly. Instead, their lives end in tremendous explosions called **supernovae.**

A relatively low-mass star (1) becomes a red giant (2). It sheds its outer atmosphere and becomes a white dwarf (3) that slowly fades into a black dwarf (4).

3

2

1

4

A star begins to die when it has used up the hydrogen in its core. How the star's life ends depends upon its mass.

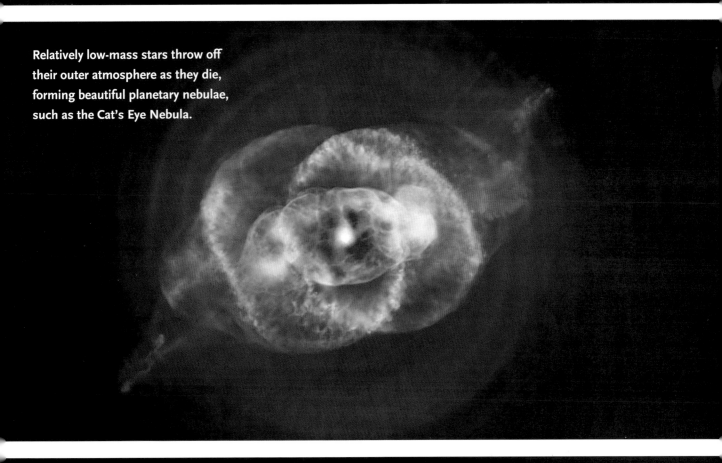

Relatively low-mass stars throw off their outer atmosphere as they die, forming beautiful planetary nebulae, such as the Cat's Eye Nebula.

A relatively high-mass star (1) becomes a red supergiant (2) and explodes in a supernova (3). It becomes either a neutron star or a black hole (4).

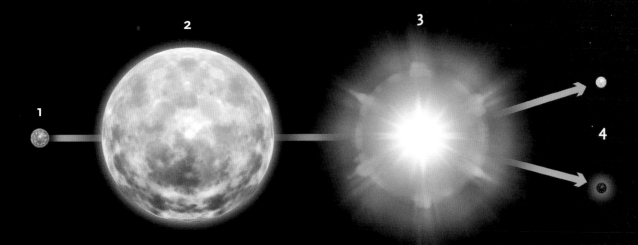

THE VARIETY OF GIANTS

Red giants are much larger than **stars** on the **main sequence.** A red giant's solar **radius** (the distance from its surface to the center) ranges from about 10 times to 100 times that of the sun. Red giants shine tens to hundreds of times as brightly as the sun does.

Red supergiants are even more extreme. At its surface, the temperature of the red supergiant Betelgeuse in the constellation Orion is only half the temperature at the surface of the sun. Yet, it is about 1,000 times as wide as the sun. It gives off about 100,000 times as much light.

THE HELIUM FLASH

As a red giant fuses its shell of **hydrogen** into **helium,** the helium falls down onto the **core.** This added **mass** causes the core to contract further, increasing its temperature. Eventually, the core begins to fuse helium into carbon. For massive stars, helium fusion begins gradually. For stars about the size of our sun, helium fusion begins rapidly in an explosive event called the helium flash.

When the red giant runs out of helium in the core, it begins to contract again. The star throws off its outer layers to form a **planetary nebula.** Eventually, all that remains is a **white dwarf.**

Betelgeuse

The red supergiant Betelgeuse forms one of the "shoulders" of the constellation Orion. Its red color is clearly visible to the unaided eye.

DID YOU KNOW?

The red supergiant Betelgeuse, the brightest star in the constellation Orion, is slowly dying. Its diameter has shrunk by about 15 percent since 1993. It may soon explode in a supernova.

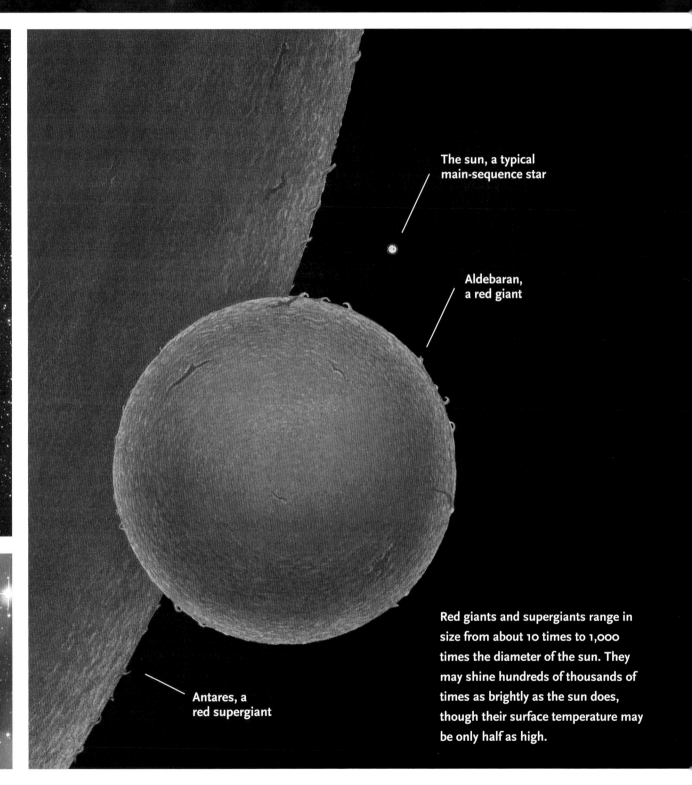

A red giant is a large, bright red star near the end of its life.

The sun, a typical main-sequence star

Aldebaran, a red giant

Antares, a red supergiant

Red giants and supergiants range in size from about 10 times to 1,000 times the diameter of the sun. They may shine hundreds of thousands of times as brightly as the sun does, though their surface temperature may be only half as high.

A SPOONFUL WEIGHS A TON

A **white dwarf** is unlike most other objects in the universe. White dwarfs typically have about 60 percent of the **mass** (amount of matter) of the sun. Yet, white dwarfs are much smaller than the sun. In fact, white dwarfs are about the size of Earth, which is tiny compared with the sun. This mystery is explained by the white dwarf's great density. Its density is about 18 tons per cubic inch (1 metric ton per cubic centimeter). Matter in a white dwarf has been crushed so powerfully that it may consist of diamond-like crystals made of carbon or oxygen.

HIDDEN COMPANIONS

A white dwarf gives off only about 1/1,000 as much light as the sun. White dwarfs are also much smaller than ordinary **stars.** As a result, no white dwarf is visible to the unaided eye. Even with telescopes, white dwarfs are difficult to detect.

THE END OF THE ROAD

A white dwarf is not necessarily white. Its color depends on its temperature. The hottest white dwarfs are violet, and the coolest are a deep red. As a white dwarf ages, it slowly cools. Eventually, the white dwarf cools so much that it no longer gives off light and becomes a **black dwarf.**

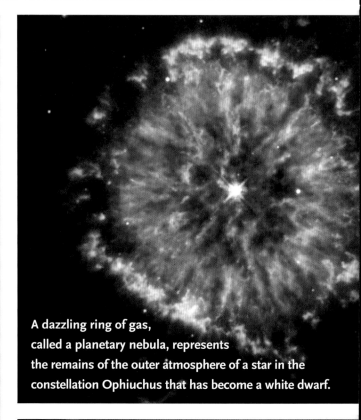

A dazzling ring of gas, called a planetary nebula, represents the remains of the outer atmosphere of a star in the constellation Ophiuchus that has become a white dwarf.

Sirius B (arrow) is the closest white dwarf to Earth. It orbits Sirius A, the brightest star in the night sky. Sirius B consists of matter 4 million times as dense as water.

A white dwarf is the hot core of a star that has used up all its fuel.

The white dwarf at the center of the planetary nebula NGC 2440 is one of the hottest known, with a temperature of 200,000 Kelvin (360,000 °F). Over millions of years, it will cool to become a black dwarf.

At the end of its life, the sun will become a red giant, swelling so much that it may consume Earth. Even if Earth survives, it will no longer be suitable for life. Fortunately, these changes will not begin for another 5 billion years.

Few things are as reliable as the sun. Each morning, it rises in the east, sharing its light and warmth with us. Each evening, it sets in the west, revealing a night sky filled with **stars.** However, like all stars, the sun will eventually reach the end of its life.

A LONG MIDDLE AGE

The **mass** of the sun allows scientists to predict when and how its life will end. The sun began to shine about 4.6 billion years ago. It has enough fuel to shine much as it does today for another 5 billion years.

The sun is only in the middle of its long life. But eventually, it will undergo violent changes.

Like other **main-sequence** stars, the sun produces energy through **nuclear fusion** of **hydrogen** in its **core.** By the end of its 10-billion-year middle age, the sun will have used up all the hydrogen in its core. It will first contract and then balloon outward, as fusion begins in a layer around the core. The sun's outer layers will be pushed far out into space. Scientists estimate that the surface of the sun may then reach nearly as far as Earth. The sun will become brighter but redder, as its surface temperature cools. It will become a **red giant.**

FROM GIANT TO DWARF

When the sun becomes a red giant, it will likely consume Earth. In any case, Earth would no longer be suitable for life. Like other low-mass red giants, the sun will eventually begin to fuse **helium** into carbon.

Gradually, the sun will shed its outer layers, forming a **planetary nebula.** Finally, fusion will shut down, and only the hot core will remain. The sun will then be a **white dwarf.** The white dwarf sun may exist for billions more years. Finally, it will cool and become a **black dwarf.** It will end its life as a dark, lifeless ball among the stars.

After it uses up all its fuel, the sun will stop glowing and become a black dwarf, a dark cinder adrift in space.

Photographs of stars in the constellation Centaurus (below) show the power of *supernovae* (exploding stars). The supernova visible in the image on the right (arrow) occurred in a galaxy so distant that it cannot even be seen in the image on the left. The supernova became brighter than some galaxies.

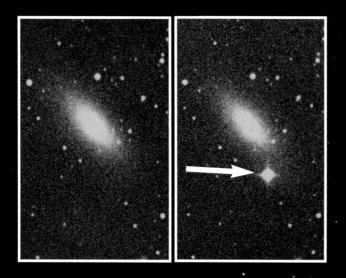

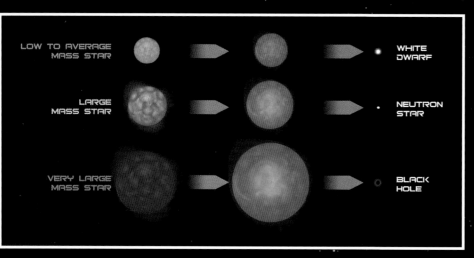

LOW TO AVERAGE MASS STAR			WHITE DWARF
LARGE MASS STAR			NEUTRON STAR
VERY LARGE MASS STAR			BLACK HOLE

◀ Stars end their lives in different ways, depending upon their mass. Relatively low-mass stars such as the sun end their lives as white dwarfs. Large stars end their lives as dense neutron stars. The largest stars end their lives as black holes, which have such powerful gravitational fields that not even light can escape.

The planetary nebula NGC 6302 (left) can be found in the constellation Scorpius, about 3,800 light-years from Earth. The nebula formed when a red giant threw off its outer atmosphere, forming two giant plumes of gas that resemble the wings of a butterfly. Once the red giant has lost all its atmosphere, only a slowly cooling white dwarf will remain.

The nearby dwarf galaxy NGC 1569 (above) is filled with bright, newborn stars. These stars may have formed when the shock waves of supernovae created dense pockets in clouds of dust and gas. The largest of these stars will themselves explode relatively soon. Shock waves from these supernovae will give rise to new stars, continuing the cycle.

Stars with relatively low **mass** (amount of matter) end their lives as **red giants,** eventually transforming into **white dwarfs.** The most massive stars take another path at the end of their lives. These stars become **red supergiants** that die in violent, incredible explosions called **supernovae.**

BRIGHTER THAN A GALAXY

When a star explodes in a supernova, it may become billions of times as bright as the sun before gradually fading from view. At its brightest, a supernova may outshine an entire **galaxy** containing billions of stars. Most supernovae reach the peak of their brightness in one to three weeks after exploding and shine intensely for several months.

The explosion throws a large cloud of gas into space at speeds of about 20,000 miles (32,000 kilometers) per second. That's 72 million miles (116 million kilometers) per hour. The mass of the expelled material may exceed 10 times the mass of the sun.

RARE BRILLIANCE

For all their power, supernovae are rare. Supernovae occur on average only once every 100 years within a typical galaxy. The last supernova in our galaxy was observed by German astronomer Johannes Kepler in 1604. Supernovae beyond our galaxy are usually too faint to be seen without a telescope. However, in 1987, an unusually brilliant supernova in a nearby galaxy was visible in the night sky for several weeks.

The next supernova in our galaxy may come from the red supergiant Betelgeuse. Betelgeuse is only about 600 **light-years** away. At such a close range, Betelgeuse's supernova would shine brighter than the moon for weeks on end.

Although supernovae occur in spiral galaxies about once every 100 years, the galaxy NGC 2770 has produced three such explosions since 1999, two of which still shine in an image taken in 2008.

SN2008D/XRF080109

SN2007uy

SN1999eh

A supernova is a tremendous explosion that marks the death of the most massive stars.

A supernova that occurred in 1987, called Supernova 1987A, was the brightest stellar explosion in nearly 400 years. Although the supernova occurred in another galaxy, it was visible to the unaided eye from Earth. The remains of the supernova are at the center of this composite X-ray and optical image.

Supernova 1987A produced powerful shock waves (above and left in an artist's illustration) that collided with and heated the surrounding gas to millions of degrees.

By the time a **star** becomes a **red supergiant**, it has already used up all the **hydrogen** in its **core.** As the core contracts and its temperature rises, the supergiant converts **helium** into carbon through **nuclear fusion.** From this point, the supergiant begins to race through its fuel, creating ever heavier **chemical elements.** Each time the fusion of a particular element ceases in the core, it continues in a thin shell surrounding the core.

DEATH BY IRON

With each heavier element, the supergiant runs through its fuel more quickly. A red supergiant with 25 times as much **mass** as the sun might fuse helium for about 700,000 years; carbon for 1,000 years; neon for 9 months; oxygen for 4 months; and silicon for about 1 day. When all the silicon in the star's core has been fused to iron, the star is doomed. Fusion of iron consumes energy instead of releasing it. As a result, fusion in the core fails, and the star collapses inward.

The Pencil Nebula, formally known as NGC 2736, is the shock wave of a supernova that occurred 11,000 years ago. The explosion threw out material from the star at 22 million miles (35 million kilometers) per hour.

DID YOU KNOW?

Chinese astronomers recorded an exceptionally bright supernova in 1054 A.D. This "guest star" was visible in daylight for 23 days.

A red supergiant creates heavier and heavier elements through nuclear fusion. When the supergiant's core becomes iron, the star collapses and explodes.

As the core collapses, its temperature rises to an astonishing 10 billion Kelvin (18 billion °F). When the core shrinks to a **radius** of about 6 miles (10 kilometers), it rebounds like a solid rubber ball that has been squeezed. This collapse and rebound occurs in less than a second.

As the core rebounds, it sends an incredibly powerful shock wave through the outer layers of the star. The energy from this shock wave causes elements in the outer layers to fuse into heavier elements. The shock wave hurls these heavier elements out into space at tremendous speed.

A star remains stable as long as the inward pull of gravity equals the pressure of radiation pushing outward from the interior (1). When a star converts the fuel in its core into iron, nuclear fusion fails, eliminating the outward pressure (2). The core collapses and then explodes with tremendous energy (3).

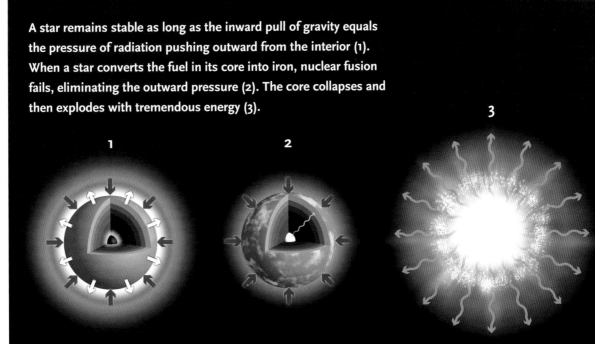

Massive **stars** die in tremendous violence, flinging material out in all directions at incredible speeds. These explosions cause new stars to be born. Life on our **planet** owes its existence to the death of a massive star.

NEBULAE AND SHOCK WAVES

When a **red supergiant** explodes in a **supernova,** it sends a shock wave through space. When this shock wave passes through the dust and gas of a **nebula,** it causes this material to clump together. It also adds many heavy **chemical elements** to the nebula. As a **protostar** forms, it gathers in many remains of the dead star. Scientists believe the **solar system** may have formed in just this way.

OUR PLANET

Much of the matter that makes up our planet was created and spread by supernovae. The interior of our planet is made up of iron and nickel. Were it not for a supernova's explosion, iron would remain locked up in dying stars. The nickel in our planet was

Modern electronics would not be possible without such heavy elements as germanium, arsenic, and tellurium. All of these heavy elements were born in supernovae.

The iron in this bridge was once part of the iron core of a red supergiant. A supernova flung the iron out into space, where it later became part of the rocks that make up our planet.

formed when a supernova shock wave ripped through the outer layers of its star. In fact, all the chemical elements heavier than iron, including such precious metals as gold, platinum, and silver, were born in supernovae. Much of the material that makes up our planet was born in the death of mighty stars.

OUR BODIES

Many of the trace metals people need to live were born in supernovae. The iron that makes our blood red in color was once in the core of a dying star. Animals such as lobsters, squids, and octopuses rely on copper rather than iron in their blood, giving it a blue color. Copper was born in supernovae. People cannot live without such trace elements as copper, iodine, and zinc. All of these metals are heavier than iron. They were created by **nuclear fusion** as a supernova shock wave passed through the outer layers of a dying star.

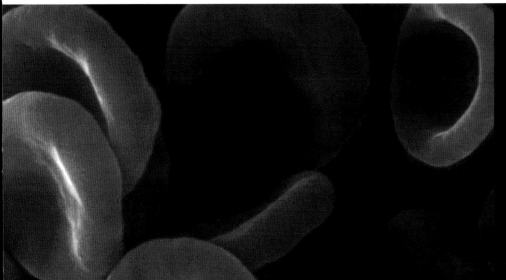

The red blood cells that give our blood its color depend upon iron to carry oxygen. Stars make iron by *fusing* (joining) the nuclei of silicon. The bluish blood of animals such as horseshoe crabs relies on copper, which is formed only in supernovae, as a powerful shock wave rips through the remains of a dying star.

Stars—Birth and Death   47

SUPERNOVAE— COSMIC FIREWORKS

The Crab Nebula was created by a bright ▶ supernova in A.D. 1054. The supernova was so bright that it could be seen even during the day. At night, it was brighter than everything but the moon, remaining visible for about two months. Today, a rapidly spinning neutron star called the Crab Pulsar is found at the center of the nebula. It is the core of the massive star that exploded nearly a thousand years ago.

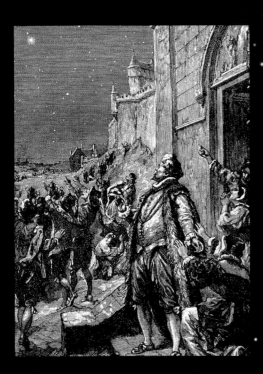

Danish astronomer Tycho Brahe observes a bright supernova in the constellation Cassiopeia in 1572. His observation helped to disprove the ancient belief that the heavens never change.

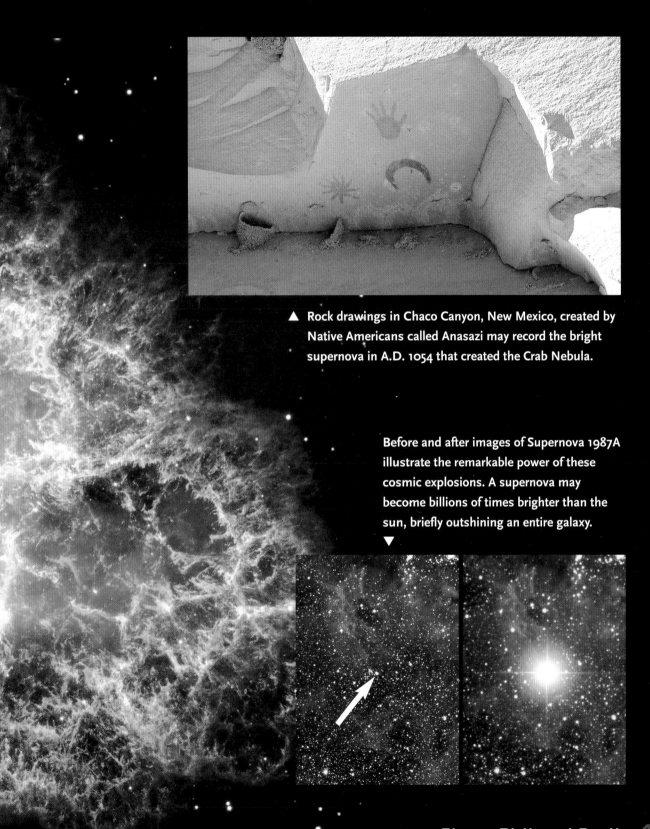

▲ Rock drawings in Chaco Canyon, New Mexico, created by Native Americans called Anasazi may record the bright supernova in A.D. 1054 that created the Crab Nebula.

Before and after images of Supernova 1987A illustrate the remarkable power of these cosmic explosions. A supernova may become billions of times brighter than the sun, briefly outshining an entire galaxy.
▼

When a **star** explodes in a **supernova,** it does not fling all of its material out into space. Despite the incredible violence of the explosion, much of the **core** remains. Many supernovae leave behind an incredibly dense, spinning body called a **neutron star.**

THE GREAT COLLAPSE

Neutron stars form from stars that originally had as much as 10 times the **mass** of the sun. Despite losing much of their material, the remaining core may be more massive than the sun, ranging from 1.4 to 3 times the mass of our own star. Neutron stars are so dense that all of this mass is squeezed into a space only 12 miles (20 kilometers) across. If taken to Earth, one tablespoon of material from a neutron star would weigh as much as 3,000 aircraft carriers. This incredible density gives neutron stars their unusual properties.

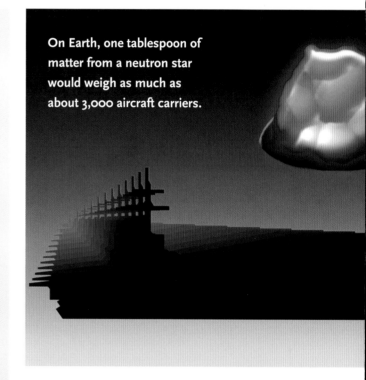

On Earth, one tablespoon of matter from a neutron star would weigh as much as about 3,000 aircraft carriers.

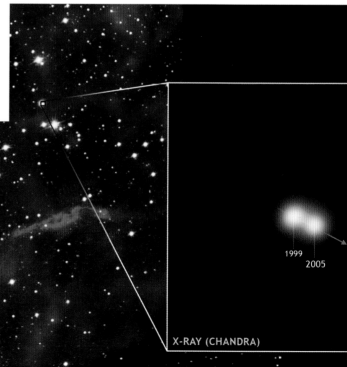

A neutron star expelled from a supernova (right) speeds away from the nebula left in the wake of the explosion. By charting the star's position over six years (inset), astronomers determined that the star is moving at more than 3 million miles (4.8 million kilometers) per hour.

1999
2005

X-RAY (CHANDRA)

A **neutron star** is an incredibly dense, spinning [star left after] a supernova.

SMASHING ATOMS

A neutron star produces a gravitational field millions of times more powerful than the most powerful magnets on Earth. This intense **gravity** smashes protons and electrons together to form neutrons. (Protons, electrons, and neutrons are tiny particles within atoms.) Scientists believe the interior of a neutron star is made up chiefly of neutrons. The surface is a solid crust of atomic *nuclei* (cores) and electrons and other particles.

SHINING X RAYS

Neutron stars have surface temperatures as high as 10 million Kelvin (K) (1.8 billion °F), though they quickly drop in temperature to about 1 million K (1.8 million °F). Neutron stars give off little **visible light.** However, they shine brightly in **X rays,** which scientists can detect with special telescopes. Astronomers first detected neutron stars by listening to the pulses of **radio waves** that some neutron stars produce. These stars are called **pulsars.**

Many neutron stars give off beams of radio waves. Because the neutron stars spin, the radio waves appear as regular pulses. Such neutron stars are called pulsars.

Some points in deep space pulse with **radio waves,** ticking as reliably as clocks. These radio pulses arrive on average twice a second, but some sources produce hundreds of bursts a second. The radio waves come from a "pulsating radio star," or **pulsar.**

COSMIC LIGHTHOUSE

Neutron stars rotate rapidly, continuing the rotation of the stars from which they were born. Just as a skater spins more rapidly if she pulls in her arms, neutron stars rotate more rapidly than their parent stars because they have shed their outer layers.

Many neutron stars produce beams of radio waves because of their powerful magnetic fields. The field rips *electrons* (negatively charged subatomic particles) and *protons* (positively charged subatomic particles) from the neutron star's surface. This process may produce beams of radio waves and other forms of **electromagnetic radiation** from opposite sides of the neutron star. Because neutron stars rotate, the radio waves arrive at Earth as pulses. Pulsars send their beams out into space like the beams of a lighthouse.

STAR CLOCK

The time it takes for a pulsar to rotate one turn is called its period. Over time, the rotation of a pulsar slows gradually. The rate at which the rotation slows is so predictable that scientists can measure time by it.

Jocelyn Bell Burnell made the first discovery of a pulsar through careful observations of radio waves from space in 1967.

DID YOU KNOW?

Astronomers think it is extremely unlikely that life on Earth could be destroyed by a supernova. A supernova would have to be within 30 light-years of Earth to produce a lethal blast of radiation, and no stars within 60 light-years are expected to go supernova within the next few million years.

A pulsar is a rapidly spinning neutron star that sends beams of radio waves out into space.

Although the Crab Pulsar shines brightly in X rays, astronomer Jocelyn Bell Burnell discovered the pulsar by observing the regular pulse of its radio waves.

When a **red supergiant** explodes in a **supernova,** much of the star's dense **core** remains. If the core's **mass** is less than about three times the mass of the sun, it forms a **neutron star.** However, if the core has a higher mass, it collapses inward until it disappears into a point. The **gravity** of this point is so intense that nothing can escape it, not even light. The star has become a **black hole.**

BENDING THE LAWS OF NATURE

Black holes are the most extreme objects in nature. Imagine the matter in a star larger than the sun squeezed down into a point much smaller than an atom. Scientists call this point a **singularity.**

Around the singularity, the black hole forms a surface called the **event horizon.** The event horizon cannot be seen or touched. Rather, it is the boundary where the pull of gravity becomes stronger than any other force. Light or anything else that reaches the event horizon disappears forever. The *radius* of the event horizon depends on the mass of the singularity at its center. (The radius is the distance from the center of a sphere to its surface.) Scientists determine the mass of a singularity by observing the orbits of nearby stars. The more massive a singularity is, the greater is its gravitational pull on these stars.

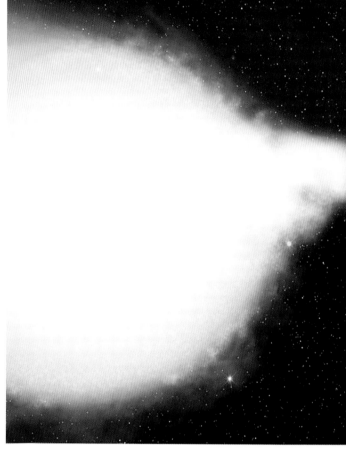

A black hole is a star that has collapsed down to a tiny point in space. Not even light can escape the gravitational force of a black hole.

Cygnus X-1 is a bright source of X rays that scientists believe could only be produced by a black hole consuming gas from its companion star, as shown in an artist's illustration.

Because light cannot escape black holes, scientists have never seen one directly. However, a black hole sometimes forms in a **binary star** system. A binary star system consists of two nearby stars that orbit around each other. In such a system, the black hole continually consumes gas from its partner star. As the gas in the **accretion disk** spirals in toward the event horizon, it becomes superheated and gives off powerful **X rays.** Using special telescopes, scientists can detect these X rays. In star systems that give off such X rays, massive stars spin rapidly around invisible partners. The partners must have tremendous mass, yet they seem to occupy no space. Scientists believe that these partners are black holes. There are likely millions of black holes in our **galaxy** alone.

A supermassive black hole at the center of galaxy M87 (arrow at left) gives off a hot jet of plasma in an image recorded by the Hubble Space Telescope.

Hot gas that radiates X rays surrounds the supermassive black hole at the center of the Milky Way Galaxy (arrow), known as Sagittarius A*.

WHAT IS A STAR CLUSTER?

The sun is part of a large **galaxy** but has no nearby companion **star**, unlike many other stars. Its nearest neighbor is several **light-years** away. However, many stars are members of large groups called star clusters.

The stars in star clusters are held together by **gravity.** Gravitational attraction causes the stars in a cluster to move through space together as a group. Individual stars within a cluster are chemically similar because they formed from the same cloud of gas. The stars in a cluster were all born at about the same time.

OPEN STAR CLUSTERS

There are two main kinds of star clusters. One kind is called an **open star cluster.** These clusters typically contain only a few hundred stars. These stars are not as tightly bound together by gravity as other clusters. In time, the cluster may be pulled apart by the gravitational force of other heavenly objects.

Open clusters are relatively young, in some cases only millions of years old. Open clusters form from the same **nebula.** Scientists think that open clusters often form because of shock waves from **supernovae.** The shock waves carry heavier **chemical elements** that were created by the supernovae. When scientists observe open clusters today, they detect signs of these heavier elements, showing that the elements became part of the stars of the cluster.

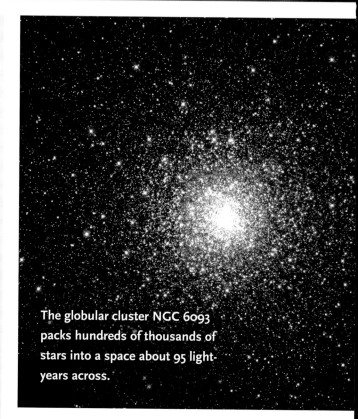

The globular cluster NGC 6093 packs hundreds of thousands of stars into a space about 95 light-years across.

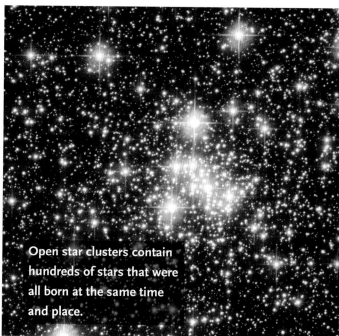

Open star clusters contain hundreds of stars that were all born at the same time and place.

A star cluster is a large group of stars that are held together by their gravitational attraction.

A second kind of cluster is called a **globular star cluster.** Many of these clusters are nearly as old as the universe, or about 13 billion years old. They contain thousands to even millions of stars in a space only dozens of **light-years** across. The stars in these clusters contain few of the heavier elements created in supernovae. Many globular clusters may have formed when colliding galaxies caused clouds of gas to collapse, setting off great bursts of star birth.

An open cluster surrounds a vivid planetary nebula known as NGC 2818, about 10,000 light-years from Earth.

Stars do not drift alone through the universe. Instead, they join with billions of others to form vast structures called a **galaxies.** Galaxies may span distances of 100,000 **light-years** or more.

SPIRAL, ELLIPTICAL, AND MORE

Galaxies come in a variety of shapes. Some are **spiral galaxies.** These galaxies are shaped like a disk, with sweeping arms of stars spiraling out from a central bulge. The disk measures from 10,000 to 100,000 **light-years** across. The stars in the arms orbit around the center, typically taking hundreds of millions of years to complete an orbit. Our galaxy, the Milky Way Galaxy, is a spiral galaxy.

Other galaxies are called **elliptical galaxies.** These galaxies may be shaped like a globe, while others are flatter. The orbits of individual stars within the elliptical galaxy determine its shape. Elliptical galaxies may form when two or more spiral galaxies collide.

Other galaxies are irregular in shape, with little organization. These galaxies tend to be relatively small, and many orbit larger galaxies.

ARCHITECTURE OF THE UNIVERSE

Few galaxies are isolated. Instead, galaxies themselves form groups containing hundreds to thousands of members. In fact, there are billions or even trillions of galaxies in the universe, each containing billions of stars.

Great filaments made of galaxies stretch across hundreds of millions of light-years in an illustration from a computer simulation.

The Milky Way is a spiral galaxy thought to resemble NGC 4321, a spiral galaxy about 52 million light-years from Earth.

A galaxy is a vast structure of stars, gas, and other matter held together by gravity.

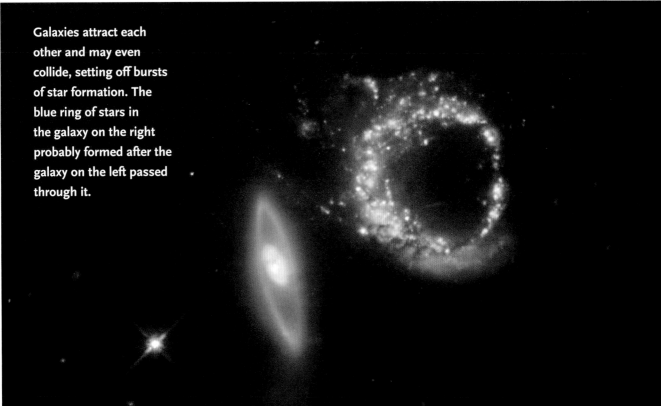

Galaxies attract each other and may even collide, setting off bursts of star formation. The blue ring of stars in the galaxy on the right probably formed after the galaxy on the left passed through it.

GLOSSARY

Accretion disk – A disk-shaped formation of gases or other interstellar matter around a massive body such as a star.

Big bang – The cosmic explosion that began the expansion of the universe.

Binary stars – Stars that orbit each other.

Black dwarf – The dark remnant of a white dwarf that has become too cold to give off light.

Black hole – The collapsed core of a massive star. The gravity of a black hole is so strong that not even light can escape.

Brown dwarf – A failed star that is larger than a planet but smaller than a true star.

Chemical element – Any substance that contains only one kind of atom.

Core – The dense, hot center of a star.

Dark nebula – A cloud of dust and gas with no stars near enough to illuminate the nebula.

Electromagnetic radiation – Any form of light, ranging from radio waves, to microwaves, to infrared light, to visible light, to ultraviolet light, to X rays, to gamma rays.

Elliptical galaxy – A galaxy with a shape that somewhat resembles a flattened globe.

Emission nebula – A cloud of dust and gas that glows because of electromagnetic radiation given off by an extremely bright star.

Event horizon – The boundary of a black hole where the pull of gravity becomes stronger than any other force.

Exoplanet – Any planet in orbit around a star other than the sun.

Galaxy – A vast system of stars, gas, dust, and other matter held together in space by gravity.

Globular star cluster – A large group of stars held together by gravity. A globular cluster may contain tens of thousands to several million stars packed tightly together.

Gravity – The force of attraction that acts between all objects because of their mass.

Helium – The second simplest chemical element. Helium is produced through the nuclear fusion of hydrogen.

Hydrogen – The simplest chemical element. Hydrogen is the most abundant substance in the universe. It fuels most stars.

Hertzsprung-Russell (H-R) diagram – A diagram that charts stars according to their *luminosity* (brightness) and surface temperature.

Infrared light – A form of light with long wavelengths. Also called heat radiation. Infrared is invisible to the unaided eye.

Kelvin scale – A metric temperature scale in which zero is absolute zero, the lowest temperature possible.

Light-year – The distance light travels in a vacuum in one year. One light-year is equal to 5.88 trillion miles (9.46 trillion kilometers).

Luminosity – The rate at which a star gives off electromagnetic radiation; brightness.

Main sequence – A description applied to any star that produces its energy through nuclear fusion of hydrogen in the core.

Mass – The amount of matter in an object.

Nebula – A cloud of dust and gas in space.

Neutron star – A star that has collapsed into a small area with extremely high mass. Neutron stars may form after massive stars explode.

Nuclear fusion – The combination of two or more atomic *nuclei* (cores) to form the nucleus of a heavier element.

Open star cluster – A group of stars held together by gravity, with younger and fewer stars than a globular cluster.

Planet – A large, round heavenly body that orbits a star.

Planetary nebula – A nebula formed when an aging star throws off its outer atmosphere.

Planetary system – A group of objects made up of a central star and orbiting planets.

Plasma – A gas-like form of matter composed of electrically charged particles.

Protostar – A ball-shaped object that has collected from the dust and gas of a nebula but has not yet become a true star.

Pulsar – A neutron star that gives off regular pulses of electromagnetic radiation.

Radio waves – The form of light with the longest wavelengths. Radio waves are invisible to the unaided eye.

Red giant – A large, bright star that glows with a reddish light. When its fuel is exhausted, a red giant becomes a white dwarf.

Red supergiant – A huge, very bright star that glows with a reddish light. When its fuel is exhausted, it explodes in a supernova.

Reflection nebula – A cloud of dust and gas typically found near a smaller, cooler star. The nebula's dust particles reflect the star's light.

Singularity – The point at the center of a black hole where the core has collapsed to a space smaller than an atom.

Solar system – The planetary system that includes the sun and Earth.

Spectrometer – An astronomical instrument that divides light into a *spectrum* (band) and records it for analysis.

Spectrum, spectra – Light divided into its different wavelengths. A spectrum may provide information about a heavenly body's chemical composition, motion, and distance.

Spiral galaxy – A galaxy with a thin, disk-like structure and sweeping arms of stars wrapped about the galaxy's center.

Star – A huge, shining ball in space that produces a tremendous amount of visible light and other forms of energy.

Stellar wind – The continuous flow of particles given off by the outer atmosphere of a star.

Supernova, supernovae – An exploding star that can become billions of times as bright as the sun before gradually fading from view.

T-Tauri star – A newborn star that has begun hydrogen fusion but is still contracting. Such stars typically throw off jets of matter.

Ultraviolet light – A form of light with short wavelengths. Ultraviolet light is invisible to the unaided eye.

Visible light – The form of light human beings can see with their eyes.

Wavelength – The distance between successive crests, or peaks, of a wave.

White dwarf – A star that has exhausted its fuel, typically no larger than the Earth but with a mass about 60 percent that of the sun.

X rays – A form of light with short wavelengths. X rays are invisible to the unaided eye.

FOR MORE INFORMATION

WEB SITES

HubbleSite Picture Album

http://hubblesite.org/gallery/

Enter the "Search Picture Album" box to find pictures of pulsars, nebulae, supernovae, white dwarfs, and other types of stars photographed by Hubble.

Pulsar Astrophysics

http://www.jb.man.ac.uk/~pulsar/Education/Sounds/sounds.html

View photographs of pulsars and listen to their sounds (by clicking on the "sounds of pulsars" link) as they were observed and recorded by the United Kingdom's radio telescopes.

Stars: A Mystery of Space

http://library.thinkquest.org/25763

Videos and interactive exercises enliven learning about the mysteries of stars.

BOOKS

Beyond the Solar System: From Red Giants to Black Holes
by Steve Parker (Rosen Central, 2008)

Death Stars, Weird Galaxies, and a Quasar-Spangled Universe
by Karen Taschek (University of New Mexico Press, 2006)

The Stars: Glowing Spheres in the Sky
by David Jefferis (Crabtree Publishing, 2009)

INDEX

accretion disks, 22, 25, 55
Anasazi, 49

Bell Burnell, Jocelyn, 52, 53
big bang, 10, 11
binary stars, 24, 30, 55
black holes, 33, 40, 54-55;
    Cygnus X-1, 55; Sagittarius A*, 55
blood cells, 47
Brahe, Tycho, 48

carbon, 10, 34, 36, 39, 44
clusters. *See* star clusters
cores, of stars, 6, 26, 39; in dying
    stars, 44-45, 54; in red giants, 34;
    in star births, 24.
    See also nuclear fusion

dwarfs: black, 9, 32, 36, 39; brown, 24,
    30-31; red, 29; white, 9, 26-27, 32,
    34, 36-37, 39-42

electromagnetic radiation, 16, 24, 52
elements, chemical, 8, 10-11, 32,
    44-45, 46
event horizons, 54
exoplanets, 29

galaxies, 10, 40, 41, 58-59; elliptical,
    58; number of, 7; spiral, 58;
    supernovae in, 42, 43
galaxies, names of: M87, 55;
    NGC 1569, 41; NGC 2770, 42;
    NGC 4321, 58.
    See also Milky Way Galaxy
gravity, 12, 20, 51, 54, 56

helium, 8, 24, 34, 39, 44
helium flash, 34
Hertzsprung-Russell (H-R) diagram,
    26-27
hydrogen, 8, 10-11, 24, 32, 39, 44

iron, 44-47

Jupiter, 29-31

Kepler, Johannes, 42

life, 11, 29, 46-47
light, 16, 51, 55
luminosity, 26-27

Magellanic Cloud, Large, 13
magnetic fields, 52
mass: in star formation, 21, 22, 24;
    of collapsing stars, 32-33, 40,
    42, 44, 50, 54; of dwarfs, 30-31,
    36; of sun, 38-39
Messier, Charles, 15
Milky Way Galaxy, 8, 14, 20, 55, 58

nebulae, 7, 18-19; dark, 16-17;
    emission, 16-17; planetary, 17,
    34, 36, 37, 39, 41, 57; reflection,
    16-17; star formation in, 12-15,
    20-22, 22, 56; true, 16
nebulae, names of: Boomerang,
    18-19; Butterfly, 8; Cat's Eye, 33;
    Crab, 48-49, 53; Eagle, 19;
    French (NGC 2736), 44-45;
    Great, in Orion, 4-5, 14-16, 22,
    25, 28; NGC 2440, 37; NGC
    2818, 57; NGC 3603, 12-13; NGC
    6093, 57; NGC 6302, 41; Pencil,
    44; Witch Head (IC 2118), 18
neutrons, 51
neutron stars, 33, 40, 48, 50-54
nuclear fusion, 6, 8, 10; in brown
    dwarfs, 30; in dying stars, 32,
    39, 44-47; in main-sequence
    stars, 26; in protostars, 24, 25;
    in sun, 39

Orion, 18, 34. *See also* nebulae,
    names of
Orion bullets, 14

planetesimals, 13
planets, 13, 28-30
plasma, 6
protostars, 12, 21-25, 30, 46
pulsars, 48, 51-53

radio waves, 51-53
red giants, 8, 9, 26-27, 32, 34-35,
    38-39, 41
red supergiants, 8, 26-27, 32-35, 42,
    44-46, 54

Sagan, Carl, 11
shock waves, 20, 21, 45-47, 56
singularities, 54
solar system, 6, 29, 46
star clusters, 56-57; globular, 57;
    NGC 6093, 56; open, 56
stars: defined, 6-7; early-stage,
    20-21; life span of, 4-5, 8-9, 12-13,
    32-33, 40; main-sequence, 25-27,
    30, 32, 39; nebulae near, 16-17;
    number of, 7; origin of first,
    10-13; planets of, 28-29;
    temperatures of, 26-27; T-Tauri,
    12-13, 24-25; where they form,
    14-15. *See also* binary stars; cores,
    of stars; dwarfs; neutron stars;
    protostars; red giants; red
    supergiants; supernovae
stars, names of: Aldebaran, 35;
    Antares, 7, 35; Betelgeuse, 34-35,
    42; Crab Pulsar, 48, 53; HE0107-
    5240, 8; LL Ori, 35; Mira, 20-21;
    Rigel, 18; RX J0822-4300, 50;
    Sher 25, 12; Sirius B, 36; T-Tauri,
    24; VB 10, 29
stellar wind, 25
sun, 6; as main-sequence star,
    26-27; life span of, 9, 32, 38-39;
    size of, 7, 35, 36
supernovae, 9, 12, 34, 40, 42-43;
    1987A, 43, 49; and Earth, 46-47,
    52; events leading to, 44-45; in
    history, 48-49; neutron stars
    from, 50; star births from, 14,
    20-21, 40-41, 56, 57; star deaths
    in, 32-33

universe, 58; expansion of, 10-11

X rays, 16, 51, 55

ACKNOWLEDGMENTS

The publishers acknowledge the following sources for illustrations. Credits read from top to bottom, left to right, on their respective pages. All illustrations, maps, charts, and diagrams were prepared by the staff unless otherwise noted.

Cover: NASA/T. A. Rector (U. Alaska), NOAO, AURA, NSF

1 NASA, ESA, and the Hubble SM4 ERO Team

4-5 NASA, ESA, T. Megeath (University of Toledo) and M. Robberto (STScI)

6-7 © Thomas V. Davis; NASA/SOHO

8-9 B. Balick, U. of Washington et al., WFPC2, HSR, NASA; NASA/Hubble/AURA/STScI

10-11 S. Beckwith & the HUDF Working Group (STScI), HST, ESA, NASA; NASA/WMAP Science Team

12-13 WORLD BOOK illustration by Debbie Mackall; Wolfgang Brandner (JPL/IPAC), Eva K. Grebel (U. Wash.), You-Hua Chu (UIUC), NASA; NASA, ESA/Hubble Heritage Team (STScI/AURA)

14-15 Gemini Observatory; C. R. O'Dell/Rice University/NASA; © Roger-Viollet, Image Works

16-17 Hubble Heritage Team (STScI) and NASA; FORS Team, 8.2-meter VLT Antu, ESO; Nick Wright (University College London), IPHAS Collaboration

18-19 NASA/STScI Digitized Sky Survey/Noel Carboni; Hubble Heritage Team, J. Biretta (STScI) et al., (STScI/AURA), ESA, NASA; NASA, ESA, and The Hubble Heritage Team (STScI/AURA); NASA/ESA/STScI/J. Hester and P. Scowen (Arizona State University)

20-21 NASA and The Hubble Heritage Team (STScI/AURA); NASA/JPL-Caltech/C. Martin (Caltech)/M. Seibert(OCIW); NASA, ESA, HEIC, and The Hubble Heritage Team (STScI/AURA)

22-23 ESO; Hong Kong University Physics Department; Hong Kong University Physics Department

24-25 C. & F. Roddier (IfA, Hawaii), CFHT; WORLD BOOK illustration by Matt Carrington; NASA and The Hubble Heritage Team (STScI/AURA)

26-27 NASA/TRACE; ESO

28-29 NASA/JPL-Caltech; C. R. O'Dell (Rice U.), NASA

30-31 Mr. Trent Dupuy and Dr. Michael Liu (Institute for Astronomy, University of Hawaii); Gemini Observatory

32-33 © Tim Brown; NASA, ESA, HEIC and The Hubble Heritage Team (STScI/AURA)

34-35 © Akira Fujii and David Malin; WORLD BOOK illustration

36-37 Space Telescope Institute/NASA and the Hubble Heritage Team; NASA, H. E. Bond and E. Nelan (Space Telescope Science Institute, Baltimore, Md.); M. Barstow and M. Burleigh (University of Leicester, U.K.); and J. B. Holberg (University of Arizona); NASA and The Hubble Heritage Team (AURA/STScI)

38-39 © Don Dixon; WORLD BOOK illustration by Matt Carrington

40-41 Palomar Observatory/Caltech; WORLD BOOK illustration; NASA, ESA, and the Hubble SM4 ERO Team; ESA/NASA

42-43 ESO/NBI/KU/CSIC/University of Hertfordshire; The Hubble Heritage Team (AURA/STScI/NASA); NASA, P. Challis, R. Kirshner (Harvard-Smithsonian Center for Astrophysics) and B. Sugerman (STScI); NASA/CXC/PSU/S. Park & D. Burrows

44-45 NASA and The Hubble Heritage Team (STScI/AURA); © Tim Brown

46-47 © David Taylor, Photo Researchers; © Shutterstock; © Microworks/Phototake/Alamy Images

48-49 Astronomie Populaire, 1884; NASA, ESA, J. Hester and A. Loll (Arizona State University); © Ron Lussier, Lenscraft; © David Malin, Anglo-Australian Observatory

50-51 NASA/CXC/Middlebury College/F. Winkler et al.; ROSAT: NASA/GSFC/S. Snowden et al.; WORLD BOOK illustration by Matt Carrington; Space Science Institute/David L. Kaplan, MIT

52-53 Independent Pictures; NASA/HST/ASU/ J. Hester et al.

54-55 Illustration by Martin Kornmesser, ESA/EC; NASA and The Hubble Heritage Team (STScI/AURA; NASA/CXC/MIT/F. K. Baganoff et al.

56-57 NASA, ESA, Hubble Heritage Team; The Hubble Heritage Team (AURA/STScI/NASA); NASA/ESA/STScI

58-59 Max Planck Institute for Astrophysics; NASA, STScI; NASA, ESA, and M. Livio (STScI)